Bloom

Brittany Seabolt

Presentation by *BookLeaf Publishing*

Web: www.bookleafpub.com

E-mail: info@bookleafpub.com

ISBN: 9789358367492

First edition 2023

To Wiley. May we always grow together.
Forever and always.

ACKNOWLEDGEMENT

Publishing this book has been a huge dream of mine. I couldn't have gotten to this point without all of the support of family and friends in my life. To my kiddos, thank you for being patient with Mommy and giving her writing time. To my best friend and husband in life, thank you for always never letting me give up on myself. You have inspired me so much more than you will ever know. I love you. To my Mom, who taught me that reading and writing are the most important things in life, and with those things, you can live a thousand lives. To my Nana and Mema, who taught me that even the smallest seeds just need patience and some time to bloom. To my other Mom, who taught me that hard work is the best way to get to where you want to be. To my friends who let me be myself, even when myself isn't the best version of me, and finally, to my Dad. I learned more from you than you could ever imagine, and I miss you every day. To my brother, thank you for being the best brother a girl could ever ask for. You have always truly been my biggest supporter. To my sisters, never change. Stay strong and stay true to who you are. I'm always here for you.

PREFACE

" I will not give up the flowers in my heart for stones just because the world is a hard place. The world is only hard because it needs more flower-hearted people."
- Nikita Gill

INDEX

You

If only you could see you, the way I see you,
then you would understand.

I see a heart refusing to give up, even though it's
been bruised and broken.
It still beats with vigorous energy, determined to
push through all the bad that has come its way.

I see ambition. Tall and unfaltering. Never
letting the negative stop its course of action.

I see kindness. The type that is rare in people
these days. Always giving and wanting better for
everyone.

I see a soul that mine fits with comfortably. Like a missing piece of myself that I didn't even know was missing until it found you.

I see a person worth losing sleep over but knowing I would never have to because you love me with an intensity that burns brighter than stars.

If only you could see you the way I do.

Hard work and Sawdust

When I was younger,
you always smelled of sawdust.
You would give me a hug as soon as you came
through the door.
I would ask you why you smelled that way.
"Hard Work", you would reply.

That's what Dads smell like I decided.

Hard work and sawdust.

Sometimes when I'm at your house,
when it's time for you to be home from work.
I look at the front door, expecting you to walk in
give me a hug,
knowing that you never will again.

In those moments
Missing you as I do
I can still faintly smell the sawdust.
As if you wrapped your arms around me,
just one more time.

Bloom

Even the smallest seed needs time to bloom.
So doesn't it make sense,
to also give yourself time to bloom.

Time to grow into the person that you want to
be.

Reflection

I have always avoided my reflection.

I'm not sure where my discomfort with it started.

Maybe, It was when I started to compare my
body to others,
that seeing the softness of my flesh and rolls and
waves of my stomach,
the fatness and fullness,
where other bodies,
the one's considered beautiful,
didn't look like mine at all

I stopped looking.

Maybe it was when I started making choices I
wasn't proud of.
When I was agreeing to things I found
uncomfortable,
making choices I knew I would later regret,
not being able to recognize who was staring
back at me from the other side.

I stopped looking.
Maybe it was when I stopped caring about my
mental health,
staring into my own eyes
as if the racing thoughts and depression could
leap out and grab me.

I stopped looking.

Now, you challenge me to look.
and I find myself, hands shaking, breathing
faster
looking into my own eyes
staring at my body
seeing into my own heart
and finding that it's ok.

It's ok to stop looking at all the imperfections
and just be.

Today I started looking.

Stardust

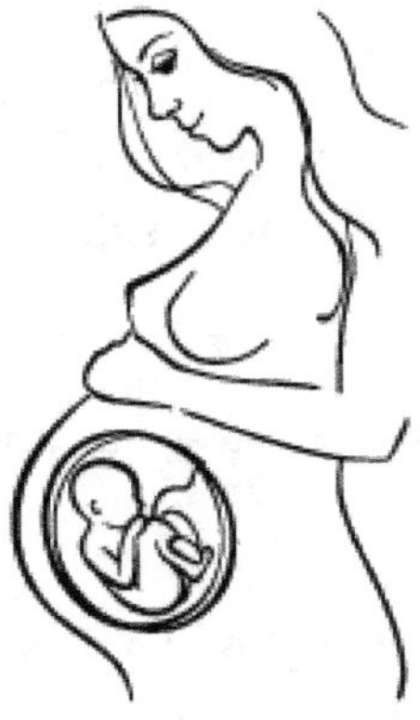

When you were born
I knew you were special.
"She's made of stardust," I said.

You have always had a way of viewing the
world through galaxy eyes.
Vast and seeing, bright and mysterious.

You see things in a way that I never could.
Where you are hopeful, I'm cautious.
Where you are kind, I'm jaded.
Where you live in a fairy tale, I have been
cemented in the ground.

I always worry that life will take you by the
shoulders and shake the clouds from your head.

That it will clear the fog from your eyes and
force you into a hard reality instead of letting
you be a dreamer.

If that happens baby girl,
Do not let them win.
Stay in the clouds
dream as high as mountains
fill up oceans with your kindness
and remember

you are made of stardust.

Daily Affirmation

May your soul be as strong as your coffee. Even if you need some sweetener to balance out the bitterness.

Backhanded Compliment

"You're so pretty for a big girl"
Well...
Why can't it be "you're pretty"?
Why does my fatness have to be acknowledged?
I'm aware of how much space I take up when I
walk into a room.
I'm aware of every roll that spills out from my
body like a waterfall.
But I will not apologize for it,
and I will not let it make me think that I am less
or unworthy.
Because I am worth every opportunity that
comes my way.
I am worth lifetimes of happiness and laughter.
I am worth love and compassion from others and
myself.
I am beautiful.

Home

Funny to imagine
that before you,
I thought I knew
what it was to be loved.
You have taught me,
that being truly, deeply, consumed
by a love like ours,
is to learn that it's different from the loves I've
had before.
Our love isn't measured by material things.
It isn't measured by dates or times.
It's infinite and boundless,
intense and burning.
Our love makes me feel,
as if my soul
has finally found home.

Advice for Positivity

You haven't truly lived until you've taken a
hurtful word and made it beautiful.
Until you've listened to another with your heart
wide open.
Until you've crossed oceans for those who
wouldn't jump a puddle for you.
Until you've sympathized with those who no
longer get sympathy from others.
Until you have dreamed wide awake, with your
light shining bright, your heart on your sleeve
and kind fierceness to your soul.

Mother Knows Best

My Mom always told me people don't like
seeing you happy and they don't like seeing you
succeed.
So, they will try to tear you down and make you
feel like you are less than you are because they
don't like how you shine.
So it's best to keep being you,
because the only person you have to impress is
yourself.

Itch

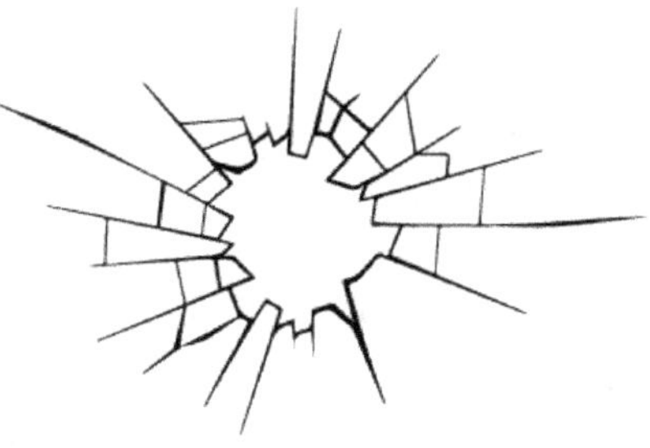

Sometimes I feel like an imposter in my own
skin.
Likes it's too tight and doesn't belong to me.

The version of myself that I feel like I am, isn't
reflected back at me.

I'm either taking up too much space or not
enough.

Oversharing or under sharing.

Awkward or too serious.

It makes me itch.

To never be comfortable
with myself.

2nd

I'm not a sore loser.
I've gotten used to being 2nd best.
I'm not the first friend in any group.
but I'm the one they call when they need a good
friend to talk to.
I'm not the best at my job,
but I always connect with just enough people to
make it feel less like a job.
I juggle a lot of things.
I'm not great at most of them but I never give up
until I accomplish my goals.
I'm ok with 2nd.
It gives you time to realize that I may not be the
first and obvious choice,
but I end up being the best one.

Rise

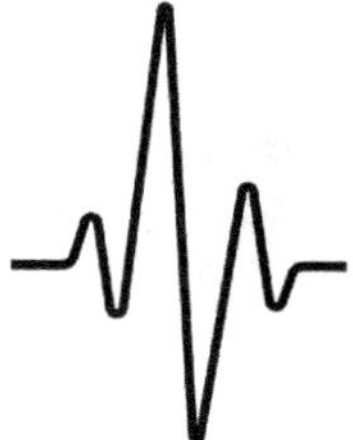

"I think I'm going to get a tattoo of a phoenix."
My Dad told me a few weeks before he passed.
In hindsight this would have been the perfect
tattoo for him
How many times did I watch him rise from the
ashes?
How many times did I see emerge from flames
seemingly unscathed?
Phoenix tears have healing powers they say,
My Dad's healing tears were his words.
There wasn't anything he couldn't help me fix
with a conversation and a hug.
I kept hoping at the time of his passing,
That he would once again, rise from the ashes
give me words of healing wisdom
and fly into the night.
But even a phoenix needs rest.

That Night

The air is thick with the promises of what can
be.
The melody of the night playing through the
trees.
We, in this moment
are infinite with possibilities.
Stars shine in your eyes as you lean over to kiss
me as softly as the breeze rustling the leaves.
No night will ever live up to that one.
The night when my soul cried out that it had
found its twin.
When my heart's tune found the melody of yours
and created a symphony of magic.
The night when no star in the sky burned as
brightly as us.

The Rabbit Hole

Follow me down the rabbit hole.
To that place where upside-down houses are
normal
and people like us are not considered outcasts,
but respectable members of society.
Where we talk in rhymes and riddles as normal
conversation,
and fantastical beasts roam the ground.
Follow me to the place where you can create in
endless loops because all your creations are
considered valuable.
That place where dreamers were meant to live.
Follow me there.

Rhyme

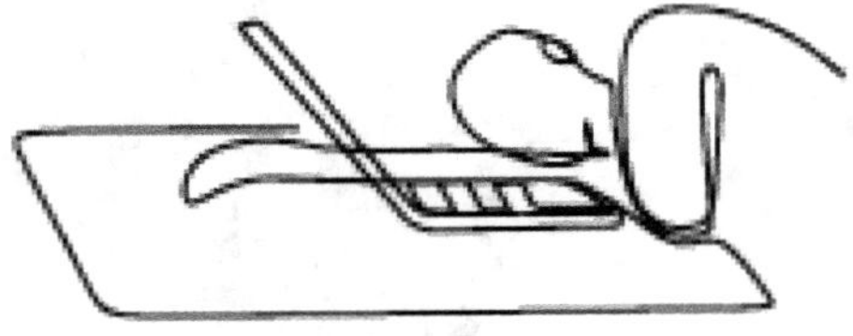

If you were the rhythm,
and if I were the rhyme,
Could the two combine?
To make a song that's unique to us,
that only we understand.
That our hearts will recognize,
when played and given a chance.

Fat Girl Problems

That feeling that you get when you have to shop
for clothes.
That defeated sigh at the selection of fabric that
never fits your body quite the right way.
You promise yourself that you will start that diet
soon.
That you will try to fit the gym into your
schedule and this won't be an issue.
You tell yourself, next summer...
Next summer I will wear "normal people"
clothes.
but next summer comes and you're faced with
the same predicament which fills you with
loathing.
You promise yourself that you will start that diet
soon...

Grow

When I grow up,
I want to change the world.

I want my words to inspire.

But not just everyone.

I want them to mostly inspire those girls who
never really fit in.

Those girls who dreamed so big but never had
the chance to chase them.

I want those girls to know that things do get
better.

That life can be unexpected but that's ok.

Adventure is part of growing and spontaneity is
part of the adventure.

There are no timelines or rules to life.

Never compare yourselves to other girls.

They aren't you.

Anxiety

Anxiety and Depression were my diagnoses at
15 years old.
They said it's why my emotions were so high.
That made sense, I guess.
I can remember the panic I would feel,
the made-up scenarios I would use to hurt my
own feelings.
The many things I decided could happen if he
didn't call me.
(The crazy thing is my intuition is so good that
most of the time I was right.)
These things were and still are hard to explain.

Why I triple-check my alarms at night because
what if I really didn't turn them on?
Why I obsess over small changes in tone or body
movement?
I think it's because I keep waiting for something
big to happen,
but I've been in flight mode for so long I don't
know how to switch it off.
So I just keep playing all these things in an
endless loop through my head.
I'm exhausted.

Dads in the South

My Dad always said that you can't accomplish anything unless you work hard to get there, and if the work gets too hard, just drink a beer and pray on it.

Seems like good advice.

Poem 21

Poem 21 is for all the dreamers with songs in their hearts and fire in their souls.

With their heads in the clouds and feet that never quite touch the ground.

To the movers and shakers that dream of the future.

Don't give up.

Keep pushing and change the world.

Be kind and always humble.

Stand up for what is right and not always easy.

Leave a place better than where you found it.